THE RIGHT TO MANAGE

CALCULATING ALLOWANCES
For Tenant Management Organisations

HMSO: LONDON

© Crown copyright 1994
Applications for reproduction should be made to HMSO
First published 1994

ISBN 0 11 752995 8

Contents

		Page
Chapter 1	**Introduction**	5
Chapter 2	**Management and Maintenance Allowances Methodology**	6

ANNEXES
	1	General Management	9
	2	Special Services	11
	3	Repairs and Maintenance	14
	4	Rents, Rates and Taxes	16
	5	Committee and Communications	17
	6	Overheads	18

Chapter 3	**Guidelines and Exemplifications**	20

Chapter 1   Introduction

The Secretary of State's guidance under regulation 7 of the Housing (Right to Manage) Regulations 1994 (SI No 627/1994) states that in drafting for the purposes of regulation 4(9) the provisions of a management agreement which determine the calculation of allowances, an approved person shall have regard to this methodology.

1.1   This document sets out the methodology to be used in calculating management and maintenance allowances for Tenant Management Organisations (TMOs) exercising the Right to Manage. It also includes exemplifications of the calculated allowance for two actual TMOs with ancillary guidance notes.

Chapter 2 Methodology

2.1   The calculation of the allowance is to be based upon the Council's own level of expenditure on the properties and functions to be taken over by the TMO.

2.2   Exceptions to this are:

(i)   Major repairs, renewals and cyclical maintenance, where a professional estimate of costs should be made for necessary work for which the Council can reasonably foresee funding being available in the light of overall spending priorities, and which the Council, in its absolute discretion, decides should be carried out.

(ii) Committee administration and training, tenant communication etc., where a flat rate payment of £20 per dwelling shall be made (including long leases/ freeholds served by the TMO).

2.3   In essence, therefore, the proposed management allowance is the sum of:

(i)   Council relevant expenditure × relevant percentage, where **Council relevant expenditure** relates to the service(s) to be managed by the TMO at the lowest hierarchical level to which they are costed, and **relevant percentage** represents the proportion of tenants/leaseholders, as appropriate, served by that relevant expenditure. The calculation of relevant percentage is weighted, for some services, by an indicator of dwelling size;

(ii) Projected costs of major works, including cyclical maintenance needed for the property to be managed by the TMO. Costs to be included are for works that the Council can reasonably expect to be able to fund, following a professional estimate of costs and taking account of other spending priorities, irrespective of whether management is vested in the TMO or the Council and which the Council, in its absolute discretion, decides should be carried out;

(iii) Number of dwellings (including tenancies and—where relevant—leaseholds and freeholds) × £20 for committee administration, training and communication.

2.4   Annexes 1 to 6 give more detail of the calculation of "relevant" percentages, and identify service divisions by reference to the standard classification of expenditure used in *Accounting for Housing*. This is a CIPFA (draft) publication giving guidance on the classification and presentation of housing accounts. When finalised, the proposed standard classification will be the recommended basis of housing accounts and CIPFA members will be required to use it, wherever possible, in preparing Council accounts.

2.5   For the purposes of these apportionments it is assumed that the cost of services provided to long leaseholders is accounted for within the Housing Revenue Account (HRA). If not, the costs apportioned to the General Fund (GF) in respect of long leaseholders will have to be "added back" to HRA costs to provide the expenditure base for the calculation of management and maintenance (M&M) allowances.

2.6 The allowance should be adjusted annually for:

(i) Changes in costs, using the adjustments in the management and maintenance allowances applied locally in HRA subsidy calculations, as effective for each individual Council (subject to an alternative option to use a different, mutually agreed index instead). The percentage applied should be the percentage after targeting (see ii below) by which the management and maintenance allowance is increased, including growth where allowed by the Department of the Environment/Welsh Office.

(ii) Efficiency savings (an annual percentage reduction for the first 5 years of a TMO's life only, the amount to be determined by the Department of the Environment/Welsh Office).

(iii) Sales under Right to Buy, rent to mortgage or voluntary sales. A flat rate reduction should be calculated, as part of the initial calculation, to be applied where a tenant purchases his/her home and becomes respectively a freeholder or long leaseholder. This will only apply where different levels of service are given according to tenure within the range of functions taken over by the TMO. The flat rate variation figures must themselves be modified each year by the percentages in (i) and (ii) above.

2.7 For those elements of the methodology based upon historic costs—actual expenditure in the last year's audited accounts (4 years for day to day repairs)—should be used *except* where significant changes to the Council's average spending levels on HRA services or management can be demonstrated by reference to approved estimates, or to current spending levels. In such circumstances, the approved estimates or current spending levels should be used as the base for the calculation (for services affected by such changes). This should also apply where:

(i) Overall spending levels have remained broadly consistent but there has been a shift in resource allocation between budget heads or cost centres;

(ii) Accounting analysis has been changed and retrospective comparisons are not possible.

2.8 The details of the calculation of the management and maintenance allowance for the TMO shall be made available to the TMO and its professional advisers, together with the supporting data which has been used to provide a basis for apportionments. The allowance calculation must be certified by the Council's Chief Financial Officer, or other qualified accountant, as complying with this methodology.

2.9 It should be noted that this financial calculation may be needed early in the Right to Manage process to enable TMOs to make an informed judgement as to the service(s) they wish to manage.

2.10 It will be open to a TMO or a Council to seek a review of the allowance where, either:-

(i) the Council's own costs have reduced significantly since establishment of the TMO's allowance; or

(ii) the rent level is set by the Council and shows an increase significantly above the level of increase (before cost savings required under the formula) applying to the management and maintenance allowance and the guideline rent for HRA subsidy purposes.

In these circumstances, the same methodology is to be used but necessarily the cost base must be established from properties remaining within the Council's management. A similar range of services, for a similar mix of properties, should be used. Where a variation in the allowance results, this should be phased in over three years. It is open to the Council and TMO to agree a shorter transition (when the Management Agreement is completed) to be applied in the event of variation.

2.11 Where an existing TMO wishes to exercise the Right to Manage for a range of services which include those currently devolved it will be necessary for a similar approach to be made. The Council and TMO must agree a similar group of properties, within the Council's management, on which to base the allowance.

2.12 It is acknowledged that extra short term costs will fall upon Councils' Housing Revenue Accounts from the establishment and funding of TMOs. The Department of the Environment/Welsh Office should be informed of the likely impact and any consequent increase in rents generally.

Annex 1   General Management

The following table sets out the standard classifications for expenditure on General Management, as being developed in *Accounting for Housing*. The "relevant expenditure" to be used for calculating the TMO allowance may include parts of contractor services or non-contractor services, depending upon the mix of functions assumed by the TMO. Less usually, the costs may include a portion of client costs where the TMO takes on a "client-agent" role. The relevant percentage is, for General Management, a straightforward percentage of tenants or lessees or both in the TMO houses as a proportion of the number of tenants, lessees or both in the whole Authority, Housing Management Area or Housing Estate. This will be calculated for the lowest hierarchical level for which costs are available.

RELEVANT EXPENDITURE AND RELEVANT PERCENTAGE		
Accounting For Housing (Main & Sub Division)	**Relevant Council Expenditure for TMO Allowance**	**Relevant Percentage %**
General Management — client costs — contractor costs — non contractor costs — TMOs [These subdivisions will include a proportion of Housing Management & Support Services (HMSS) costs.]	Lessee only services Costs for services taken on by TMO (normally contractor costs only but could include client costs where role undertaken).	$100 \times$ No of leaseholds in TMO No of leaseholds in Authority/Area/Estate
	Tenant only services Costs for services taken on by TMO (normally contractor costs only but could include client costs where role undertaken).	$100 \times$ No of tenancies in TMO No of tenancies in Authority/Area/Estate
	Services to all residents Costs for services taken on by TMO (normally contractor costs only but could include client costs where role undertaken).	$100 \times$ No of units in TMO No of units in Authority/Area/Estate

Notes:

1. Until the new standard form of accounting is fully implemented it will be necessary to include costs within the present heading "Supervision and Management—General" but exclude:

    (i) those parts of central and support costs falling within the proposed definition of "Service Strategy and Regulation" (see annex 6); and

    (ii) those costs which relate to client services for CCT except insofar as the TMO is to act as the client's agent for particular services—i.e. in contract specification and monitoring.

2. These distinctions, and the choice of options within the *TMO Modular Management Agreement*, make it probable that apportionment of management costs will be necessary. As staffing costs are the major element of these costs, it is recommended that an analysis of staff time and cost be undertaken between activities relevant to the TMO and those not relevant. Front line management activities, at area or estate office (or whole authority for smaller Councils), together with direct support operations relevant to a particular service element (e.g. legal services for debt recovery or rent collection), must be identified. Other less targeted Housing Management and Support Services should be allocated pro rata to identifiable staff/HMSS costs. Office costs should similarly be allocated pro rata.

3. Where office costs do not include rent (because the offices are freehold) an "asset rent" should be professionally calculated and added into the relevant expenditure, in lieu of any relevant debt charges.

4. Care needs to be taken to ensure that the base costs include the full cost of Non-Domestic Rate (i.e. excluding any relief) where the TMO will not qualify for relief, or 20% only where the TMO will qualify for 80% relief.

5. Pension costs must similarly be on a "like for like" basis. In circumstances where the Council's contribution to the Superannuation Fund has been reduced to reflect past surpluses (e.g. a contribution holiday), or increased to meet accrued liabilities, the base should be adjusted to reflect the normal level of contributions.

6. Where the costs of General Management include costs of holding and servicing committee meetings (even after excluding service strategy and regulation costs or communication with tenants) these costs may be excluded from relevant expenditure. This is to avoid "double counting" as these items are covered by the flat rate, per dwelling, allowance.

Annex 2 Special Services

The following table sets out the standard classifications for Special Services as being developed in *Accounting for Housing*. The relevant expenditure on which the TMO allowance is to be based will include all costs for the services taken on by the TMO. The relevant percentage is a calculation of the TMO dwellings as a percentage of Housing Management Area, Housing Estate, or Block. The calculation will be made separately for each service at the lowest hierarchical level at which costing information is available.

Because these services will vary in cost, to some extent, in proportion to the size of the building or the number of residents, the apportionment is based upon "weighted" units—with larger flats/houses counting in the apportionment more than small flats/houses.

RELEVANT EXPENDITURE & RELEVANT PERCENTAGE		
Accounting For Housing (Main & Sub Division)	**Relevant Council Expenditure For TMO Allowance**	**Relevant Percentage %**
Special Services		
— Heating — Communal lighting — Lifts — Laundry Services — Caretaking — Cleaning — Grounds Maintenance — Warden Services — Other	All costs—but for services to be managed by the TMO only.	<u>100 × weighted dwellings in TMO</u> Weighted dwellings in Area/Estate/Block (calculated separately for each service to reflect the number of dwellings in the TMO receiving the service as a proportion of those in the Housing Management Area or Housing Estate or Block receiving the Service). [See note 5]

Notes:

1. Where a TMO takes responsibility for only part of a service (and where that sub service is not separately costed) it will be necessary to break down costs between sub services having reference to contract specifications/tenders, time sheets or other documented evidence of the best apportionment.

2. It is expected that the above services will apply equally to tenants and leaseholders. If not, separate calculations of the relevant percentage will be needed.

3. For services not applying to all dwellings within the TMO or the Area/Estate or Block to which costing information is available the number of dwellings included in the numerator and/or denominator of the relevant percentage calculation must only be those receiving that particular service.

4. Weighted dwellings units should be calculated as follows:-

 1 bedroom — weighted unit = 1

 2 bedrooms — weighted unit = 1½

 3 bedrooms — weighted unit = 2

 4 bedrooms — weighted unit = 2½

 (and so on).

5. In some circumstances, the Council may have access to a demonstrably better apportionment base than weighted dwelling units. This is particularly likely where contract specifications have been drawn up by reference to particular properties or by area measurement. Where this is the case, and documentary confirmation is available, such data should be used in preference to the generalised basis above.

6. Similarly, where a TMO is to "buy back" services from a Council, the element of "allowance" for the service concerned may be amended to match the "price" payable by the TMO.

7. Note 3 above makes it clear that where services are not provided equally to all dwellings in the TMO or the Authority/Area/Estate/Block the numerator and denominator used to calculate the relevant percentage should only include dwellings receiving the service. An extension of this principle is important for heating services where dwellings with different heat sources will have different unit costs. To calculate the element of the allowance for heating it may be necessary to make separate calculations for each group of properties served by different heat sources.

8. Where sewerage, cesspool or costs of treatment works are relevant these should be included as follows:-

 (i) *First time rural sewage*
 Where properties within the TMO have been connected to mains sewerage recently and debt charges remain payable, a view must be taken as to whether this is an element of capital financing (outside the Right to Manage). If the TMO is taking responsibility for payment (to the Council or the water company) an equal element of allowance must be made.

 (ii) *Cesspool Charges*
 Where the TMO is served by cesspool(s) which are emptied, at a charge, by the water company, the actual charge made by the water company, and payable by the TMO, must be included in the allowance.

 (iii) *Sewage Treatment Works*
 Where the TMO takes responsibility for the operation of sewage treatment works serving TMO properties, the full running costs should

be included in the allowance. Where separate costs centres are not used, and such costs are aggregated Council wide, the aggregate cost should be apportioned, as set out in note 3 above.

Annex 3 Repairs & Maintenance

The following table sets out the standard classification for expenditure on repairs and maintenance as being developed in *Accounting for Housing*. For TMO allowance calculation purposes, different treatment is proposed for day-to-day or general maintenance, which is likely to have a fairly consistent expenditure level, year-on-year, and cyclic and structural repairs which clearly do not.

For the former, relevant expenditure is proposed as a four year average, at the lowest available costing level, for the aspects of repairs to be taken on by the TMO. For the latter, a professional estimate is needed, to forecast expenditure levels.

The relevant percentage should be calculated for general repairs etc on a weighted basis, as for special services, with separate calculations for elements of repairs which do not apply uniformly to all residents (e.g. in-flat repairs, lessees only).

RELEVANT EXPENDITURE & RELEVANT PERCENTAGE		
Accounting For Housing (Main & Sub Division)	**Relevant Council Expenditure for TMO Allowance**	**Relevant Percentage %**
<u>Repairs & Maintenance or Repairs Fund Contribution</u>		
Day-to-Day/General Repairs & Maintenance (including internal decorations)	4 year average expenditure (including management of repairs)	$\dfrac{100 \times \text{weighted dwellings}}{\text{Weighted dwellings in Block/Estate/Area}}$
Cyclic Repairs (including external decorations and structural repairs)	Professional Estimate of work required (include fees and in-house management cost) for which the Council can reasonably foresee funding being available and decides should be carried out.	See note 8

Notes:

1. Day to day repairs will need further breakdown to distinguish between work done for tenants and long leaseholders, and separate calculations made of "relevant percentage".

2. Where a particular type of work is carried out for some tenants only (e.g. internal decorations for elderly only) a refined percentage calculation using weighted numbers of eligible tenants only may be used.

3. Under the *TMO Modular Management Agreement*, it is possible for the TMO to select, for its management, certain trade skills only. It is anticipated that some Councils will have costing data for different trade classifications. If not, a qualified surveyor will need to advise on the appropriate split for the TMO properties, or alternatively, a statistically valid sample of repair notes/jobs may be taken to provide a realistic apportionment.

4. The four year average expenditure needs to be calculated at a constant price base. The Department of Environment/Welsh Office percentage applied locally for increased costs in the HRA subsidy calculation (as defined for uprating purposes in this methodology) should be used, unless a more closely relevant index is agreed between the TMO and the Council, to adjust to current price levels.

5. In some circumstances, the four year average may be obviously distorted by exceptionally high or low expenditure in one year. In these circumstances it is suggested that five years' figures are extracted and the highest and lowest (after uprating) excluded from the average.

6. Where improvements or other major works have been, or will be, carried out and these have an impact on responsive maintenance costs, that impact should be assessed (by a qualified surveyor) and added or deducted from the allowance.

7. As for special services, it is recognised that some Councils may have access to a demonstrably better apportionment base than weighted dwelling units. Where this is the case, and documentary confirmation is available, such apportionment base should be used in preference to the generalised basis above.

8. For major works, including cyclic repairs or renewals, it is necessary for the Council to consider:

    (i) the work required to maintain the property condition or to bring it to S.11 standard; and

    (ii) the resources which might reasonably be expected to be available to carry out such work, taking into account the Council's spending priorities.

9. Where the TMO has elected to take responsibility for major works, a professional estimate of the cost which can foreseeably be funded should be made.

10. By agreement between the Council and the TMO, the funds allocated for the major works may either be paid to the TMO as an annualised element of the methodology or in the form of profiled payments which match the incidence of costs falling upon the TMO.

11. It needs to be recognised that estimates for major repair works can prove inadequate when a more detailed survey is undertaken prior to specifying and letting the contract. In these circumstances, the TMO may seek additional resources from the Council under chapter 2 sub-clause 6.2 option C of the *TMO Modular Management Agreement*.

Annex 4 Rents, Rates and Taxes

The following table shows the standard classifications for expenditure on Rents, Rates, Taxes and other charges. Expenditure on Lease Rentals or Rates/Water Rates on non-dwellings should be identified explicitly for TMO properties (in which case the relevant percentage is, self-evidently, 100%).

Council Tax on vacant property is best taken at authority wide level and apportioned pro-rata to the number of units.

RELEVANT EXPENDITURE & RELEVANT PERCENTAGE		
Accounting For Housing (Main & Sub Division)	**Relevant Council Expenditure for TMO Allowance**	**Relevant Percentage %**
<u>Rents, Rates, Taxes and Other Charges</u>		
Lease Rentals	Actual expenditure on TMO property	100
Council Tax on Vacant Property	Actual expenditure council wide	$\dfrac{100 \times \text{No of TMO tenancies}}{\text{Total tenancies in Authority}}$
Rates/water rates on non-HRA dwellings	Actual on TMO properties	100

Notes:
1. Lease rental expenditure is only to be included where the TMO takes responsibility for payment.

Annex 5 Committee and Communications

Notes:

1. The allowance for committee and communication expenses is to be calculated as:

    No. of dwellings (tenants and—where appropriate—leaseholders/freeholders/voids) × £20.

2. This allowance is intended to cover the costs of annual meetings, committee administration and training, committee members' expenses and the costs of publishing and distributing information to tenants as required under the *TMO Modular Management Agreement*.

3. Where the TMO provides services to freeholders, they should be included in the number of dwellings above.

4. Where a Council agrees, a higher rate per dwelling may be paid.

Annex 6   Overheads

Notes:

1. The definitions in *Accounting for Housing* of "Service Strategy and Regulation" and "Housing Management and Support Services" are consistent with similar CIPFA publications *Accounting for Education* and *Accounting for Social Services*. They are therefore unlikely to change in final versions but, of course, are not yet implemented.

2. Until such time as the draft CIPFA document is finalised it is useful to confirm the type of costs that should not rank within the base cost for calculating the TMO allowance. For the avoidance of doubt, therefore, the following costs, although a proportion may currently be charged to the Housing Revenue Account, should be **excluded** from the relevant expenditure base for calculating allowances:

    (i) *Corporate Management*
    - Meetings of the Council and of corporate policy-making committees and attendance at them, so far as they are not also responsible for the management of Housing Revenue Account related services;
    - The salaries and expenses of mayors and chairmen of Councils and their respective deputies;
    - Chief executives (except to the extent of any time which they spend directly on specific services or DSOs for which they are personally responsible);
    - Officers designated under section 114 of the Local Government Finance Act 1988 and section 5 of the Local Government and Housing Act 1989, when carrying out their duties under those sections;
    - Estimating and accounting for precepts, block grants and Councils' own shares of rates and community charges and work on standard spending assessments;
    - Preparing and publishing statements of accounts, corporate budgets and all-service annual reports;
    - Subscriptions to local authority associations and attendance at their conferences and meetings;
    - Flat rate allowances paid to members;
    - Local elections;
    - The staff, accommodation and services needed to support the meetings, personnel and activities described above.

    (ii) *Regulation*
    - Duties which Councils are required by statute to carry out in order to maintain the standard of services to the public, either by their own employees or by third parties;

- ◆ Shadow regulation, which comprises those activities which are currently carried out as part of the management of directly managed service units, to the extent that these activities would have to continue in order to comply with statutory requirements if the service units were to be sold, or if any part of their management were to be delegated;
- ◆ Chief officers with a statutory responsibility for the management of a particular service.

(iii) *Strategy*

- ◆ Periodical review of local housing needs (Section 8 of the Housing Act 1985), but not reviews under Section 605 as the benefits can be identified directly to particular functions. This category includes all the work relating to strategic information, research and information which is necessary *up to the point* where strategic planning for specific divisions of services is possible;
- ◆ Preparation of the housing budget; but only so far as the activities are concerned with the limited series of specific tasks involved in determining the overall size of the housing budget, its allocation to service heads and preparation and presentation of revenue and capital estimates to the housing committee.
- ◆ Preparation of reports and returns to the Department of the Environment or Welsh Office relating to strategic matters; for example, the collation of information provided by service divisions to complete the HIP1 return;
- ◆ Liaison with outside bodies for strategic planning purposes;
- ◆ Costs necessitated by the duty to have regard to environmental considerations before taking any action under the Housing Act 1985 (Section 607);
- ◆ Shadow regulation of directly managed service units; the costs of management, to the extent that the regulation of the functions performed would have to remain with the Council in order to comply with statutory requirements if the activities were no longer performed directly.

In calculating the element of cost to be excluded from central and departmental charges, before the above definitions come into general use, it is necessary for Council finance staff to examine working papers to identify the element of charge relating to activities within this list. Where this is not immediately apparent, an estimate of the time split between SSR and HMSS must be made in consultation with the charging department or section. Where timesheets are available these should be analysed to support the estimated split.

Chapter 3   Guidelines and Exemplifications

3.1   This chapter shows the components of allowance calculation for two actual Tenant Management Organisations.

3.2   For the sake of confidentiality they are referred to as Council/TMO 'X' and 'Y'.

3.3   The exemplifications have regard to the following notes which explain the adjustment from gross Council costs to relevant expenditure for TMO allowance calculation.

3.4   **General Management**
Note 1
Where the TMO does not undertake a complete Housing Management role, it is necessary to include only those relevant activities in the allowance calculation. Any adjustment (illustrated under "TMO Apportionment" as "Relevant %') will need to be based on timesheet evidence, examination of job descriptions or management assessment.

Note 2
Costs not relevant to TMO activity should be eliminated from the allowance calculation. They will normally relate to support services and other functions operated and managed centrally.

Note 3
Service, Strategy and Regulation (SSR) costs as defined in *Accounting for Housing* should be quantified by reference to timesheets, job descriptions or other assessment and excluded from appropriate cost centres before the allowance calculation is made.

Note 4
Insurance of dwellings premiums should be excluded from the allowance calculation as these (as would be usual) remain the responsibility of the Council.

Note 5
Right to Buy Administration is normally operated as a central function and a TMO would only be involved in receiving and passing on applications. Normally, total exclusion would occur. If the TMO did undertake any such duties involving quantifiable expenditure, apportionment would be based on the ratio of leaseholders.

Note 6
Service Level Agreements will have been made for the supply of many Housing Management Support Services. Related costs should be examined and non-relevant and central strategic (SSR) elements eliminated before allowance calculations are made.

3.5 Other Items

Note 7

Certain special services (e.g. Ground Maintenance) may contain an element which is managed centrally rather than being devolved to estate or area level. A proportion of such costs should be apportioned to the TMO using the standard weighted methodology. Non-TMO relevant costs should be eliminated before apportionment.

Note 8

Client Services Units may be set up by the Council to control and administer contracts for various special services. Where the TMO undertakes some or part of these activities, costs will need to be apportioned to it using the standard weighted methodology after non-relevant costs have been excluded.

Note 9

Some costs will vary dependent on circumstances. For instance, the level of Heating expenditure will reflect the source of supply and tariff applicable to it. Disaggregation of costs should be undertaken bearing this in mind and the resultant figure apportioned on the basis of dwellings containing the same type of fuel and installation to ensure equity of treatment.

eg	Heating—District	£
	Total costs	7,239,937
	Deduct non-relevant costs	985,577
	Revised cost	6,254,360
	Total Dwellings involved	19,174
	Total Weighted Dwellings	33,013
	TMO Dwellings involved	20
	TMO Weighted Dwellings	31

$$\text{Allowance} \quad 6{,}254{,}360 \times \frac{31}{33013} = £5873$$

Note 10

Other special services (e.g. Lifts, Cesspool Emptying in Rural areas) may not apply throughout the Council's dwelling units, being confined to blocks or areas benefiting from the service applied. Where such costs are held at a level above the TMO, apportionment should be based on weighted dwelling units served or number of installations involved as appropriate.

Note 11

Certain expenditure will apply only to rented dwellings so apportionment must exclude leased dwellings. Some examples where this will arise are Council Tax Void payments and Day-to-day Repairs.

Note 12

Where estate office costs do not include rent, a notional "asset rent" calculation will need to be undertaken and added to relevant expenditure.

Note 13

Special services cover those items listed in the standard methodology. Exclusions need to be made for functions not undertaken by the TMO or chargeable to it. In the illustration, items where recoverable income is received direct by the Council have been excluded.

Note 14

Some activities will need to be apportioned according to different criteria to that set out in the standard methodology dependent on the level at which costs are held and the distribution of the activity within the Council. Where these costs are not directly allocated, apportionment should be based on the numbers or types involved. Examples are Club Rooms and Community Centres which may only be provided in some areas.

Note 15

Where any Day-to-day Repairs expenditure is retained by the Council, these costs should be excluded before apportionment to the TMO is made.

Note 16

Planned Maintenance generally is carried out over the whole of a Council's area or estate so apportionment of the allowance should be made on the basis of total weighted TMO and Authority or estate dwelling numbers.

3.6.1 COUNCIL "X"

Cost Detail Head	Note	Actual Cost	Adjustment	Revised Cost Current Year	TMO Apportionment Rel %	TMO Apportionment Amount
BASE YEAR—1994/95 BUDGET						
Cost Level—Authority Wide						
General Management	1					
CCT Team	2	237,700	237,700			
Hostels	2	145,600	145,600			
Head Office	2&3	2,602,900	1,849,200	753,700	27	203,499
Strategy	2	414,100	414,100			
Development	2	204,500	204,500			
Central Lettings Service	2&3	132,200		132,200	27	35,694
TOTAL		**3,737,000**	**2,851,100**	**885,900**		**239,193**
Grounds Maintenance		588,000		588,000		
Cleaning & Caretaking	2	240,500	89,400	151,100		
TOTAL		**828,500**	**89,400**	**739,100**		
Cost Level—Neighbourhood						
Area Office Costs		138,400		138,400		
Sheltered Units	2	21,100	21,100			
Responsive Repairs		117,100		117,100		

3.6.2 COUNCIL "X"

Stock Numbers		1 Bed 1.00	2 Beds 1.50	3 Beds 2.00	4 Beds 2.50	Total	Weighted units
Authority	Tenant Lessee	10,806	9,184	10,425	504	30,919	46,692
Area Incl.	Tenant Lessee						
Estate Incl.	Tenant Lessee	196	85	215		496	754
Block Incl.	Tenant Lessee						
TMO	Tenant Lessee	96		95		191	286
Special Services							

3.6.3 COUNCIL "X"

Relevant Percentage	No of Registered Units				Relevant Percentage			
	LA	Area	Estate	Block	TMO	TMO/ LA	TMO/ Area	TMO/ Estate	TMO/ Block
Total Number Tenant Lessee									
All	30,919		496		191	0.617743		38.5081	
Total Weighted Tenant Lessee									
All	46,692		754		286	0.6125525		37.9562	
Special Services Relevant to Part of TMO									

3.6.4 COUNCIL "X"

Note:-
Relevant expenditure represents the cost of services to be taken over by the TMO at the lowest costing level available uprated to present price levels where appropriate.

	Relevant Expenditure Costed to					TMO	
	LA £'000	Area £'000	Estate £'000	Block £'000	Source	%	Allowance £
General Management CCT Team	0				94-95 BUD	0.6177431	0
Hostels	0					0.6177431	0
Head Office	203,499					0.6177431	1,257
Strategy	0					0.6177431	0
Development	0					0.6177431	0
Central Lettings Service	35,694					0.6177431	220
Ground Maintenance	588,000					0.6125246	3,602
Cleaning & Caretaking	151,100					0.6125246	926
Cost Level—Neighbourhood							
Area Office Costs			138,400			38.50806	53,295
Sheltered Units			0			37.95620	0
Responsive Repairs			117,100			37.95620	44,447
Committee & Communications						20	3,820
Total Allowance							107,567
Allowance per dwelling							563

3.7.1 COUNCIL "Y"

Cost Detail Head	Note	Actual Cost	Adjustment	Revised Cost
Base Year—1994/95 Budget				
<u>Cost Level—Authority Wide</u>				
General Management	1			
Directorate	2	401,882	329,666	72,216
Training & Personnel	2 & 3	587,180	135,618	451,562
Central Administration	3	389,764	317,217	72,547
Finance	2 & 4	2,213,232	2,113,232	100,000
Rent Accounting & Recovery	2 & 3	1,200,371	643,036	557,335
Right to Buy	5	813,229	813,229	
Service Level Agreements	6	7,823,635	5,484,187	2,339,448
Information Technology	2	1,445,183	1,121,597	323,586
TOTAL		14,874,476	10,957,782	3,916,694
Other Expenditure				
Client Services Units	8			
Ground Maintenance	7	46,925		46,925
Management	2	93,540	93,540	
Cleaning	2	106,335	53,168	53,167
Building	2	208,996	104,498	104,498
Heating—District	9	7,239,937	985,577	6,254,360
Heating—Individual	9	397,199	79,440	317,759
Lifts & Electrical	10	1,044,687	208,937	835,750
Special R & M	2	543,308	362,308	181,000
Programming	2	172,644	172,644	
Out of Hours Services	2	113,908	22,782	91,126
Council Tax Voids	11	208,000		208,000
TOTAL		10,175,479	2,082,894	8,092,585
<u>Cost Level— Neighbourhood</u>				
Office Costs	12	868,391	10,639	879,030
Special Services	13	964,515	360,880	603,635
Club Rooms	14	7,395		7,395
Day to Day Repairs	11 & 15	1,963,306	68,716	1,894,590
Planned Maintenance	16	581,643		581,643

3.7.2 COUNCIL "Y"

Stock Numbers	1 Bed 1.00	2 beds 1.50	3 Beds 2.00	4 Beds 2.50	Total	Weighted Units

Authority
    Tenant
    Lessee
	19,928	21,359	17,389	1,305	59,981	90,007

Area Incl.
    Tenant
    Lessee						

Estate Incl.
    Tenant
    Lessee
	957	1,315	843	16	3,131	4,656

Block Incl.
    Tenant
    Lessee						

TMO
    Tenant
    Lessee
	479	604	364	12	1,459	2,143

Special Services Relevant to part of TMO
Heating—District
    Borough
    TMO
						33,013
						31

Heating—Individual
    Borough
    TMO
						52,521
						1,914

Lifts & Electrical
    Borough
    TMO
						1,271
						50

Club Rooms
    Neighbourhood
    TMO
						9
						1

Day to Day Repairs
    Neighbourhood
    TMO
						4,325
						2,011

Council Tax Voids
    LA
    TMO
					54,970
					1,336	

3.7.3 COUNCIL "Y"

Relevant Percentage	No of Registered Units					Relevant Percentage			
	LA	Area	Estate	Block	TMO	TMO/LA	TMO/Area	TMO/Estate	TMO/Block
Total Number Tenant Lessee									
All	59,981		3,131		1,459	2.43244		46.5985	
Total Weighted Tenant Lessee									
All	90,007		4,656		2,143	2.38093		46.0316	
Special Services Relevant to Part of TMO									
Heating—District	33,013				31	0.09390			
Heating—Individual	52,521				1,914	3.64426			
Lifts & Electrical	1,271				50	3.93391			
Club Rooms			9		1			11.1111	
Day to Day Repairs			4,325		2,011			46.4971	
Council Tax Voids	54,970				1,336	2.43042			

27

3.7.4 COUNCIL "Y"

Note:-
Relevant Expenditure represents the cost of services to be taken over by the TMO at the lowest costing level available uprated to present price levels where appropriate.

	Relevant Expenditure Costed To				Source	TMO	
	LA £'000	Area £'000	Estate £'000	Block £'000		%	Allowance £
General Management							
Directorate	72,216				94-95 BUD	2.432437	1,757
Training & Personnel	451,562					2.432437	10,984
Central Admin.	72,547					2.432437	1,765
Finance	100,000					2.432437	2,432
Rent Acctg & Recovery	557,335					2.432437	13,557
Right to Buy						2.432437	
Service Level Agreements	2,339,448					2.432437	56,906
Information Technology	323,586					2.432437	7,871
Other Expenditure							
Grounds Maintenance	46,925					2.432437	1,141
Management						2.432437	
Cleaning	53,167					2.432437	1,293
Building	104,498					2.432437	2,542
Special R & M	181,000					2.432437	4,403
Programming						2.432437	
Out of Hours Services	91,126					2.432437	2,217
Social Services							
Heating—District	6,254,360					.0939024	5,873
Heating—Individual	317,759					3.644257	11,580
Lifts & Electrical	835,750					3.93391	32,878
Council Tax Voids	208,000					2.430417	5,055
Neighbourhood Costs							
Office Costs			879,030			46.59853	409,615
Special Services			603,635			46.03158	277,863
Club Rooms			7,395			11.11111	822
Day to Day Repairs			1,894,590			46.49711	880,930
Planned Maintenance			581,643			46.03158	267,739
Committee & Communications						20	29,180
Total Allowance							2,028,401
Allowance per Dwelling							1,390